DEE'S BIG NUTS

Written by
Mark Thunder

Dee was a squirrel who had big nuts.

His nut sack was so big...

that it would drag on the ground everywhere he went.

Dee had a friend named Sarah who loved nuts.

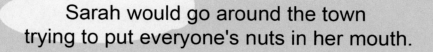

Sarah would go around the town
trying to put everyone's nuts in her mouth.

Sarah loved how big Dee's nuts were. His nuts were her favorite.

They were the biggest nuts she had ever seen!

She would play with his nuts all day and sometimes even at night.

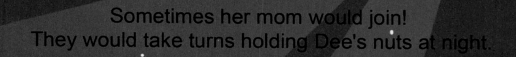
Sometimes her mom would join!
They would take turns holding Dee's nuts at night.

Sometimes Sarah would even try to put both of Dee's nuts in her mouth at the same time.

She would giggle, her face would turn red and
then his nuts would come flying out!

One day, someone ran up to his nuts and started poking them!

Although Sarah loved Dee's nuts, she would sometimes kick them.

She once kicked them so hard, she busted a nut!

Dee was very sad that Sarah busted his nut.

He just wanted Sarah to play nice with his nuts.

One day when his nuts were feeling better, she took them to lunch,

where she got peanut butter all over them! His nuts were so sticky.

After that day, she knew she would need to play nice ...

because all good squirrels know how to play nice with big nuts!

The End.

Sit back and enjoy this children's book parody about a squirrel named Dee and his friends love for his big nuts. Each page will have you laughing and going nuts! This may look like a typical children's book but once the book opens, you will enjoy references that only adults will understand.

Dee's Big Nuts makes a great gift for birthdays, anniversaries, bridal shower, wedding gifts, housewarming gifts or just a great gift to make a friend or loved one giggle in laughter.

ISBN 9781515326762

90000

9 781515 326762

Usborne Baby's World

Baby's toys